Martin Van Buren

A Captivating Guide to the Man Who Served as the Eighth President of the United States

Free Bonus from Captivating History (Available for a Limited time)

Hi History Lovers!

Now you have a chance to join our exclusive history list so you can get your first history ebook for free as well as discounts and a potential to get more history books for free! Simply visit the link below to join.

Captivatinghistory.com/ebook

Also, make sure to follow us on:

Twitter: @Captivhistory

Facebook: Captivating History:@captivatinghistory

Contents

Introduction

History chiefly remembers Martin Van Buren (December 5, 1782 - July 24, 1862) as the eighth president of the United States (1837–1841). He was also, however, notable for achieving many firsts in American politics. He was the first American president to be born a citizen of the country, and not a British subject[i]. (The American Declaration of Independence from British rule took place on July 4, 1776, a mere six years before he was born[ii]). He was the first Dutchman and the first man without Anglo-Saxon ancestry to serve as president. He was the first and only American president to have been raised in a language other than English. He was also the first New Yorker to ascend to the Oval Office in the White House, at a time when Manhattan was becoming the urban heart of a future America (as it is today). Historians have also recognized him as the first "professional politician" to occupy the presidential seat. His expressed capacity for political intrigue, strategic pragmatism and politically expedient "non-committalism" has earned him his fair share of critics and detractors.

The legacy that Van Buren left behind is marked by his position as one of the founders of the Democratic Party and a creator of the modern political system. His shrewdness as a tactical politician is well-documented. Unlike world-famous American presidents like Abraham Lincoln, John F. Kennedy, or Woodrow Wilson, Van Buren made no grand and memorable speeches that galvanized and inspired the nation with a noble and lofty vision of an ideal America. Instead, he was referred to as the "Little Magician" to his allies and the "Sly Fox" (or "The Red Fox of Kinderhook") to his enemies; each moniker casted his political acumen in a different light. His other nicknames include "The Enchanter", "The Careful Dutchman", "Little Van", "The Great Manager", and "the American Talleyrand". This profusion hints at the difficulties many observers faced in pinning down his true ideological stance and character as an individual. The elusiveness of his character is also noted in this 1835 poem by Davy Crockett:

"Good Lord! What is VAN!–for though simple he looks,

Tis a task to unravel his looks and his crooks;

With his depths and his shallows, his good and his evil,

All in all, he's a Riddle *must riddle the devil[iii] "*

The "little" descriptor references his height (five feet and six inches) – an anomaly in a nation that has consistently preferred to vote for much taller presidential candidates[iv]. In political cartoon illustrations of the time, Van Buren is almost always depicted wearing an impeccable and well-fitting suit, an allusion to his reputation for being a dandy. With his short stature, balding head, and prominent sideburns, he was often unfavorably compared – physically and politically – to his predecessor Andrew Jackson.

His political career is marked by two clear chapters: the rise and the fall. Despite being born to a father who worked as a farmer and tavern keeper, Van Buren became exposed to the world of law and politics at a very early age. His father's tavern was a hotspot for political discussion and debate, attracting prominent figures such as Alexander Hamilton (one of the Union's Founding Fathers) and Aaron Burr (the third American vice president who famously killed Hamilton in a duel in 1804). Given his relative poverty, Van Buren did not attend college. He opted instead to become a legal apprentice when he was only 14 years old. A year later, he won his very first court case.

His career as a New York lawyer served him well for an early start in politics. He served two terms in the New York State Senate (1812 – 1820) and was elected as the state attorney general from 1815 to 1819. After mastering political control of the most populous state in the Union, he took to the grander stage of national politics when he was elected to the U.S. Senate in 1821[v].

There, he became the leading figure of the Albany Regency: one of America's first political machines. This efficient state political organization helped him secure votes, make deals, generate strategic publicity, and exert a powerful influence over New York and national politics. After Van Buren secured the trust of Andrew Jackson, another lawyer-turned-politician who became the first leader of the Democratic Party, his ascent to the White House was sealed[vi]. When Jackson became the seventh president of the United States in 1829 (he ran with Van Buren as his nominee for vice president), Van Buren was appointed Secretary of State. Jackson and Van Buren's alliance remained strong throughout his four years in office, ensuring that he was handpicked by Jackson as his successor during the 1836 presidential elections.

Once he had assumed the highest political position in the country, however, Van Buren faced one setback after another. During his Inaugural Address, he triumphantly characterized America as a successful nation that the rest of the world should emulate. The enviable prosperity he described would be cruelly short-lived.

The financial crisis that struck the nation just after he assumed office in 1837 (known as the "Panic of 1837") was the worst economic crisis the then-relatively young nation had endured. Furthermore, his administration would pay the costs of a prolonged war with the Seminole Indians of Florida during his tenure. He also lost popular support when he decided not to support the annexation of the newly independent - and slave-owning - state of Texas. In 1840, he failed to be re-elected for a second term when William Henry Harrison secured an overwhelming majority of the votes.

When he attempted to secure the Democratic presidential nomination in 1844, Van Buren found that his refusal to support the annexation of Texas had decisively cost him the endorsement of Southern delegations. He still ran for president as a candidate of the newly-formed Free Soil Party[vii], but he ultimately failed to win even a single state (he won 10% of the votes).

His political career may have ended in defeat, but his life was certainly not a tragedy. After retiring from public life, Van Buren spent a few years living and traveling in Europe. He began to write his lengthy autobiography in Italy ("At the age of seventy-one, and in a foreign land, I commence a sketch of the principal events of my life"). It was only published much later on, as what is arguably the nation's first presidential memoir, in the 1920s. He eventually returned to his Lindenwald estate, in his hometown of Kinderhook, to live out the final years of his life.

He witnessed the controversial and divisive question of slavery tear the entire nation apart in his final years. At the ripe old age of 79, he passed away – over a year after the American Civil War (1861 – 1865) broke out and Abraham Lincoln was elected as the 16th president of the United States. His wife and cousin, Hannah Van Buren (née Van Alen) had died much earlier in 1819 (he never remarried). He was succeeded by four children.

Sandwiched between Andrew Jackson and the American Civil War, history may find it difficult to remember Van Buren. It may tend to dismiss him as simply being of the nation's many "average" presidents, an unfair label for any president whose tenure coincided with a major economic depression.

When Van Buren lived, however, the entire American population (which numbered at 17 million during the 1840 Census) had an opinion on him. Van Buren may not be associated with inspiring American ideals, but he paved the way for a then-unprecedented democratic mechanism. He stands alongside Grover Cleveland, the

22nd and 24th president of the United States, and one of the two American presidents who secured the presidency without a college education or military career. Born without privilege, Van Buren dared to oppose the interests of the wealthy as a lawyer and a politician even when he knew it would be costly to do so.

The darkness of his times (the first depression, the question of slavery, the forceful relocation of Native American tribes from their ancestral lands) easily come to mind, but America was also hurtling towards the future we live in during Van Buren's reign. The seeds of the modernity we recognize so well – railway networks, democracy, the printing press – were sowed in his era. Six small townships and cities – in Maine, Kentucky, Indiana, Missouri, Ohio, and Arkansas – still bear his surname. To understand the history of American politics, one must understand Van Buren's often overlooked legacy.

Chapter 1 – Early Life

Van Buren was born on December 5, 1782, in the village of Kinderhook, Columbia County, New York. The small town, which had been settled before 1651, was strategically located on the east bank of the Hudson River and twenty miles south of Albany, the capital city of the state of New York and an early political hub[viii]. Like Albany, Kinderhook was a predominantly Dutch settlement. Van Buren's father, Abraham Van Buren, and his mother, Maria Hoes Van Alen, were both of Dutch descent. Van Buren was the third child (out of five); he also had a half-sister and two half-brothers from his mother's first marriage.

Their little personal history could prompt an observer to foresee that Martin Van Buren would amount to political greatness. The Van Burens had been living in Kinderhook since 1631, after deciding to abandon Holland and cross the Atlantic Ocean. At the time, the American Dream involved the idea of a productive career in agriculture and a large, ever-growing family. The Van Burens amassed no larger businesses or swaths of land; they remained in Kinderhook for over a hundred years as a tight-knit community. Instead of marrying into other European settler communities, they married among themselves. In his autobiography, Van Buren would boast that there was no intermarriage in his ancestry – from the arrival of the first Van Buren to his son's marriage – across two centuries and six generations.

Abraham Van Buren had waited until he was 39 to settle down. He was not the most financially shrewd or calculative man, but he had amassed enough money to keep his family in the middle of the social hierarchy. As with twenty-five percent of the community, he owned slaves (6 altogether). Van Buren thus grew up as the middle child amongst eight siblings, living in an overcrowded one-and-a-half-story wooden tavern.

With five children and three stepchildren to support, Abraham Van Buren worked two jobs: a farmer and tavern keeper. After attending classes at the village school and, later on, the Kinderhook Academy, Van Buren would help his father build a fire every day and execute periodic cleaning duties. This opened up a new world for the young boy – a world apart from the idyllic, slow-paced, religious, insular, and farming-based small town he grew up in.

The tavern provided informal learning opportunities that would help him on his ascent to the highest office in the country, as it was a popular meeting place for noteworthy politicians and lawyers. Kinderhook lays strategically on the highway between Albany in the south, and Boston and New York in the north. As lawyers, politicians, and businessmen made their way to and from these bustling urban centers, many stopped for a comfortable night or two at Abraham Van Buren's tavern. Apart from playing host to them and their worldly concerns, it served as the local polling spot during elections.

Van Buren was born just five years after the 4th of July; his earliest memories were filled with dreams of revolution, independence, conflict, and the promise of a future greatness. As one of the original thirteen colonies that form the Union (Delaware, Pennsylvania, New Jersey, Georgia, Connecticut, Massachusetts Bay, Maryland, South Carolina, New Hampshire, Virginia, North Carolina, and Rhode Island and Providence Plantations), New York was an old state even then. It still attracted immigrants and travelers, always promising to evolve and grow instead of remaining stagnant.

As the tavern-owner's son, Van Buren felt insecure when he had to encounter the political and social elites of his time. These were men with great reputations and wealth – men who dwelled in large mansions and owned sweeping amounts of land. These were men like New York Republican Aaron Burr, a charismatic and famous political figure. His parents were by no means impoverished, but they still had to work hard for their livelihoods while being confined to small-town existence.

At the young age of fourteen, Van Buren became a legal apprentice to a local lawyer named Francis Silvester. His father's wealth had shrunk as he grew up, leaving him unable to support his children's education financially. Despite being a bright student, he had to navigate life without the confidence and security that comes from having completed his formal education. From early on, he learned about the importance of maintaining a fastidious image when Silvester complained about Van Buren's dirty clothes and unkempt appearance.

Apart from demonstrating an impressive intelligence and eloquence at this stage in his life, Van Buren showed a willingness to endure social disapproval for sticking to his political beliefs. His employer was a member of the Federalist Party, an early national American political power that maintained power from 1789 to 1801[ix]. It stood for the newly written Constitution and the federal character of the proposed Union of states while opposing the idea of a republican government and the French Revolution. When Silvester's father was elected as the state senator, Van Buren alienated his employer and townspeople by refusing to join in the festivities. Despite the taunts, abuse, harassment, and ridicule, his destiny to be a Democrat had been decided early on.

One door closed; another opened. His political inclinations captured the attention of John and William Van Ness, members of another influential family that supported Thomas Jefferson's championing of individual freedom as the core essence of the American Revolution[x].

After Van Buren helped John Van Ness secure a nomination to Congress, they sent him to New York City to study and live with William, a rising Republication lawyer.

What did New York City offer to Van Buren when he arrived there as a young man, only 19 years of age, in 1801? At the beginning of the 19th century, New York City was on its way to becoming the largest city in America – home to famed figures like Washington Irving[xi] (America's first writer of national prominence), John Jacob Astor (America's first millionaire), legendary journalist and New York Tribune editor Horace Greeley, Cornelius Vanderbilt ("The Commodore", owner of an entire fleet of steamboats), and famed Detective Thomas Byrnes[xii].

William Van Ness' personal connection to Vice President Aaron Burr[xiii] allowed Van Buren to access Tammany Hall[xiv]: a social club that evolved into a political machine that dominated much of New York City in the 1800s. This was a time when the Federalists were losing their grip on political supremacy – and a time when Van Buren was personally acquainted with the vice president of the United States. Given their closeness and physical resemblance, people begin to suspect that Burr was Van Buren's biological father.

If there is any truth to this, it did not stop Van Buren from voting against Burr when he ran for the position of governor of New York as an independent candidate in 1803. Van Buren had passed the bar, and began to practice law in Kinderhook. Meanwhile, he became a keen observer of the intense political battles that took place between the Federalists and Republicans. Meanwhile, democratic principles flourished during Thomas Jefferson's two-term reign as America's third president.

Jefferson's leadership affirmed Van Buren's democratic convictions. In his memoir, he wrote "My faith in the capacity of the masses of the People of our Country to govern themselves, and in their general integrity in the exercise of that function, was very decided and was more and more strengthened as my intercourse with them extended.[xv"] He admired Jefferson's untiring efforts to entrench a democratic worldview despite opposition from the wealthy elite and the printing press.

Chapter 2 – The Skilled Lawyer

While his political ambitions were put on hold, Van Buren's legal practice and family grew. He married his first cousin Hannah Hoes on February 21, 1807, staying true to his family's tradition of intermarrying. Little is known about Hoes, partly because of her early death in 1819 – after giving him four sons. Van Buren did not mention her in his lengthy autobiography, but the fact that he never remarried after her death suggests that he was either not much of a romantic or never met someone who could replace her.

Before Hoes' death, the future looked bright. The opening of a new water highway had shortened the travel time (by steamboat) between New York City and Albany. To take advantage of the business opportunities on offer, Van Buren relocated his practice to the new and bustling town of Hudson. This decision paid off – he was soon making $10,000 a year and establishing his reputation as one of Hudson River's most brilliant attorneys.

During the 19th century, lawyers were not seen as opportunistic money-makers. Instead, they embodied lofty ideals of justice and rightness, with their mastery of Latin, parchments, and position above the realms of ordinary men. Van Buren had been scoffed at because of his appearance in the past (and would continue to be scoffed at as he grew older), but in the courtroom he commanded respect and admiration with his sharp memory, impeccable research skills, and implacable common sense.

The courtroom was his battleground, a chance to hone and refine his oratory and rhetorical skills. His arch-rival appeared in the form of Elisha Williams, a firm Federalist and supporter of the elite families that Van Buren fought against in court. Williams could dismiss Van Buren's humble origins and his height, but it was much more difficult for him to take down Van Buren's judgment, analysis, and well-honed skills of persuasion. As time progressed, Van Buren began to win a greater proportion of their legal scuffles. Those who continued to underestimate him would pay, as Van Buren now had the resources to address his disadvantaged background. He purchased a law library from another attorney, and made up for his lack of formal schooling by devouring its contents at night.

The farmer's son from Kinderhook was now in the company of social and economic elites, but he never turned his back on the lower and middling class that ushered him into the world. He took a wide range of cases that came his way, but in time one could see a clear pattern. He opposed the interests of the small number of wealthy families in favor of the smaller and more numerous freeholders. Van Buren's intentions were not entirely noble. He loved the thrill of winning, and he also loved the victory over the Federalists who believed that they had the natural capacity to govern everyone since they could not possibly govern themselves. With their lands, money, pride, and a history of victory, his opponents' defeat caused much rage and indignation.

Van Buren's legal career was soaring, but he also had another, greater ambition. In 1812, his established reputation as a defender of people's rights earned him a narrow victory when he ran for state senate. He defeated two wealthier candidates to secure the Republican nomination. He was only twenty-nine years old, making him the second youngest senator ever to have been elected in New York.

Chapter 3 – The Albany Regency

Van Buren began his term in the New York Senate in 1812, on a momentous date: the Fourth of July. His timing was excellent. New York was poised to become the dominant center of American politics, a position it would then retain for over a hundred years.

Furthermore, the War of 1812 had erupted just a month before, on June 18[xvi]. The French revolutionary and Napoleonic Wars had pitted France against Britain since 1792, compromising American economic interests in the process as each country attempted to prevent it from trading with its opponent. America had been politically divided between the pro-French Republicans and the pro-British Federalists, with the Republicans gaining an upper hand when Thomas Jefferson was elected in 1801. By 1809, American and British relations had deteriorated to the point of Congress implementing the Non-Intercourse Act, which banned any form of trade with France and Great Britain.

The war was widely supported by Americans from the western and southern fronts (who were vehemently jingoistic and wished to prove America's might against its former colonial master), but it served to disrupt the commerce that the New Englanders relied on. When James Madison (the 4th American president and Jefferson's successor) declared war on Great Britain, New York was placed at the forefront of British military aggression.

The conflict and chaos nevertheless presented Van Buren with the opportunity to shine. He had voiced his opposition to British interests before, and now he could oppose them in the name of the idea of a republic America, New York, and democracy. The idea of a population being able to govern themselves now stood against the prominent British example of an aristocratic form of government. He was willing to put money and manpower where his mouth was. He advanced the Classification Bill, which aimed to allow New York to conscript 12,000 white men who were between eighteen years old and forty-five years old to fight for the nation's ideals. It was not actually implemented (the war ended in early 1815), but it had been hailed as "the most energetic war measure ever adopted in our America" by Thomas Hart Benton[xvii].

The boost in reputation that Van Buren received from the popularity of the bill helped him to advance his political career. Apart from the transferable skills he had gained from his years practicing law, his ascent was also aided by his amiable personality and capacity for hard work (he woke up at 4:30 am every morning).

One of Van Buren's key political contributions was to alleviate the plight of cash-poor rural folk. At the time, farmers and small businessmen who failed to repay their debts were placed in prison. Van Buren argued that this practice amounted to a jail sentence "for the misfortune of being poor, of being unable to satisfy the all-digesting stomach of some ravenous creditor[xviii]". He also opposed the proposed re-chartering of the Bank of the United States in 1812 since this would concentrate financial resources in the hands of a small number of men (this would primarily benefit the Federalists).

Van Buren knew that he did not have the powerful charisma of previous American leaders like Alexander Hamilton[xix] or Aaron Burr. What he had was the foresight to create a smooth-functioning political machine that would allow him to capture the loyalty of New York's large and ever-increasing population. The political character of the previous era – where success depended on personal influence and the massive wealth of great families – was coming to an end. In its place, Van Buren would impose discipline, meritocracy, uncompromising loyalty, and meticulous political positioning.

Before Van Buren could reach the top of the New York political ladder, he had to deal with the competition. His primary rival was the confident and visionary DeWitt Clinton[xx], the mayor of New York and an ex-senator. Clinton was a man of wealth, but he supported Jeffersonian ideals[xxi] when it was time to vote. This meant a belief in the rights of the individual states vis-à-vis the Federal government, an uncompromising interpretation of the federal constitution, a conviction that the common people had the knowledge and capacity for politics, and a focus on an agrarian (and not a commercial or industrial) economy. Clinton and Van Buren were initially political allies, but in time they began to see each other as arch-rivals. With his formidable organizational skills and his ability to think, speak, and behave strategically, Van Buren eventually outmaneuvered his more capricious rival after approximately a decade of political competition.

Meanwhile, Van Buren had succeeded in attracting many bright and enthusiastic lawyers and journalists who would support him and comply with his leadership. His early followers included men such as William L. March, John Edmonds, Benjamin Butler, and Silas Wright. These men became Van Buren's closest friends and supporters; their alliance eventually evolved to become a sophisticated political organization with a defined party ideology and a knack for manipulating the press to advance their interests.

They were described via several names – e.g. "the Bucktails" and the "Holy Alliance" – before they became widely known as "the Albany Regency". Thurlow Weed, the young journalist who coined the descriptor, stated "I do not believe that a stronger political combination ever existed at any state capital, or even at the national capital. They were men of great ability, great industry, indomitable courage, and strict personal integrity[xxii]." The Albany Regency aimed to advance Jeffersonian principles while reckoning with New York's rapid economic growth.

On February 5, 1819, Van Buren suffered the death of his wife Hannah. At only thirty-six, he became a widower with four sons. With his parents both long departed, there were no close family members around to console him and help him look after the children. To make matters worse, his arch-rival Clinton had been elected governor of New York in 1817. When Van Buren made a reach for the attorney general position, Clinton effectively stopped him.

Furthermore, the thorny question of slavery[xxiii] had become unavoidable. As Missouri was poised to enter the Union, New York Congressman James Tallmadge suggested that the state be barred from increasing its number of slaves. The conflict of interests (ideals vs. economics) between the North and the South would dominate the political fabric until Van Buren's death. Between 1815 and 1861, the Northern economies were modernizing and diversifying, moving away from agriculture and investing in canals, roads, railroads, steamboats, banking, insurance, printing presses, newspapers, and magazines. On the other hand, their Southern counterparts had less of an incentive to move away from producing labor-intensive cotton, which skyrocketed in value in the 1850s. Tobacco and sugar were two other lucrative products from the slave-run plantation economy. Slaves were more economically valuable than machines in the South, and the wealthy Southerners did not think twice about using their wealth to influence national politics in their favor.

The number of wealthy plantation-owning white men may have been few, but their lesser privileged neighbors harbored ambitions of becoming similarly wealthy through the very same means[xxiv]. In 1850, there were only 347,525 slaveholders (out of a total white population of about 6 million in the slave-owning states). Only half of them had more than four slaves (and were thus potentially plantation operators). Less than 1,800 men owned over a hundred slaves. The ideology that blacks were innately inferior to whites and needed to be "civilized" by slavery, however, was certainly widespread in the South – and even in many Northern communities.

Van Buren aligned himself with the anti-slavery movement in New York at this time but was not wholly devoted to the cause. While his opposition to slavery angered the slave-owning elites, he was also criticized for failing to attend an important meeting on the Missouri question and thus not being able to sign the anti-slavery document that was agreed on there.

Van Buren was nevertheless poised to rise to political eminence in New York. By 1820, the Albany Regency had become highly adept at navigating the political scene. In 1821, Van Buren managed a hard-won victory when he ran for the U.S. Senate. After that, his allies gained control of the state council of appointment, allowing them to effectively control the patronage of New York. They also introduced a proposal to rewrite the state constitution, which favored Clinton's mode of autocratic government. The changes they introduced increased the number of voters to 260,000, shortened the governor's tenure from three to two years, championed party rule over individual rule, and reformed the judiciary and patronage systems. Van Buren opposed those who wanted to deny African Americans voting rights but then agreed that they should own $250 before being allowed to vote – which effectively prevented many of them from stepping into the voting booth.

Together, these changes established the fact that the American Revolution did not end on the 4th of July. Revolution was a continuous work in progress, and democratic ideals had to be constantly fought for. As Van Buren's power soared in New York, New York's status in the Union grew with its population and economic activity. It was time for Van Buren to set his sights on the national political stage.

Chapter 4 – Washington

Van Buren had mastered the New York bureaucracy and secured victory against his competitors, but the national political stage was a different beast altogether. Would his talents and experience be sufficient for his success here?

In November 1821, the month Van Buren arrived in Washington, the city was a far cry from its today's glorified position as the seat of political power in the United States of America. The White House still suffered burn marks from the 1814 fire, and the Capitol building was still under construction. There were only 23,000 people living there, with 7,000 of them being slaves.

The lack of splendor and opulence did not hinder Van Buren, who quickly became acquainted with his new neighbors. He did, however, face a grave setback when he delivered his first speech in the Senate. While attempting to debate about a Louisiana land transaction, he suffered a breakdown and lost his bearing through his speech. He did, however, recover from the humiliation by winning the subsequent debate with an adversary.

In time, Van Buren's championing of Thomas Jefferson's antiquated ideals helped him be elected as the chairman of the Judiciary Committee – a position that would allow him to reinvent the entire nation's political system. Diary entries from Charlemagne Tower, his New York acquaintance, revealed that Van Buren had plans to resurrect the old Democratic Party despite only being a first-year senator[xxv]. The messiness of the national political order stood in his way, especially with the blurring of ideological boundaries between the Republicans and the Federalists.

Van Buren began to recreate the trappings of the Albany Regency on the national stage. Alliances had to be built, a disciplined platform needed to materialize, and he needed to tap into his loyal base in New York to secure the respect from the other states in the Union. Van Buren imagined a tightly scripted communication network from the leaders of the party to state chairmen to local committees. As the son of a tavern keeper, he also knew that politics could be social, lively, fun, and habit-forming.

He thus helped create the two-party democracy system that Americans take for granted today. There is actually no mention of two parties in the Constitution[xxvi]; the Founding Fathers had presumed that this would lead to violence, conflict, and an unproductive rivalry. They had rather naively presumed that the ideals of democracy would spread automatically across the nation because political visionaries such as themselves had imagined it.

In truth, however, the presence of active opposition parties has now become a critical indicator of an emerging democracy. Van Buren is not widely credited for advancing the idea that a two-party system is needed to create a balance of power, but he did effectively build the system that would allow it to exist in the United States – and other countries that emulated it – from the time it emerged in 1828.

How he built that system is a matter that eludes historians and even his peers. Van Buren built the Democratic Party, but the exact steps, manoeuvers, and decisions he made along the way are mostly invisible, occurring behind the scenes of his public appearances as a politician. What is more readily known is his capacity to be the life of the party with his charming and social nature. As mentioned previously, Van Buren never remarried, but he was known for his fondness for the ladies of Washington. He could flatter, amuse and chat with the wives of his contemporaries, but somehow never suffered from the taint of a scandal. His favorite female social companion was said to be Ellen Randolph, the granddaughter of Thomas Jefferson, but no evidence of any romantic dalliance remains – if there was any to begin with.

The Northern politician gained popularity with his Southern counterparts by virtue of his gregarious nature and political stance. They all agreed that government expansionism and the Supreme Court should be checked, that banks should be regulated, and improvements should be localized, and that anything that was not specified in the Constitution should be weeded out. Southern politicians like John Taylor, William Crawford, and Nathaniel Macon began to ally themselves with Van Buren. Thomas Ritchie, an intellectual and influential editor that controlled Virginia the way Van Buren controlled New York with the Albany Regency, soon became a close personal and political friend – signaling the dawn of a powerful New York and Virginia alliance.

Van Buren also courted the favor of the political giants of the past. In May 1824, he spent several days with Thomas Jefferson in Monticello, Virginia. Their mutual affinity raised eyebrows in Washington. Van Buren also visited John Adams at his estate in Quincy, Massachusetts.

When James Monroe's term as the fifth president of the United States drew to an end in 1824, Van Buren decided to support Georgia's Willian H. Crawford. Van Buren began marshaling his networks and resources to support his nominee, but Crawford himself suffered a paralytic stroke that thwarted the campaign to get him elected. In the end, John Quincy Adams[xxvii] was elected the sixth president – a severe blow to Van Buren's political ambitions.

The ascendancy of New York left an opposite impact on his spirits. The Erie Canal was completed in 1825[xxviii], connecting the Hudson Valley with the Great Lakes (Lake Ontario and Lake Eerie). It cost $7 million but would provide significant economic gains to the entire state of New York. It was the first canal to connect the western waterways to the Atlantic Ocean, and would serve as a precedent for other great engineering feats in the country. Virginia was once the Union's most populous state; by 1820 New York was in the lead with over a million inhabitants. It contributed $16 million to the Union's annual custom receipts of $27 million in 1825. Its political value would only rise to match its unparalleled economic value.

During Adams' presidency, Van Buren allied himself with Andrew Jackson[xxix]. They began to form a political alliance that would oppose some of the Adams administration's policies. The network of alliances that came into being was anything but accidental – Van Buren meticulously looked for strategic allies in the form of politicians and journalists from all corners of the Union. In time, Amos Kendall (Kentucky), Francis Blair (Kentucky), Isaac Hill (New Hampshire), James Buchanan (Pennsylvania), and Thomas Hart Benson (Missouri) rallied around Jackson and Van Buren. Van Buren imagined a national party bound by principles instead of personalities, which would help alleviate the sectional divisions over the question of slavery. On January 13, 1827, he wrote a letter to Virginian political mastermind Thomas Ritchie to outline his vision:

"the effect of such a nomination of Gen'l Jackson could not fail to be considerable. His election, as the result of his military services without reference to party & so far as he alone is concerned, scarcely to principle, would be one thing. His election as the result of a combined and concerted effort of a political party, holding in the main to certain tenets & opposed to certain prevailing principles, might be another and a far different thing[xxx]."

The "far different thing" that he prophesied – the Democracy – eventually came into being. Under President Adams' nose, a vast, growing, and powerful new political entity slowly stepped away from the shadows into the public field of vision. Adams certainly recognized the threat posed by Van Buren; he described him as "the great electioneering manager for General Jackson", and compared him to Aaron Burr's role in national politics between 1799 and 1800.

As the 1828 election drew closer, Van Buren and Andrew Jackson began to set aside their political differences to carve out a common ground. When DeWitt Clinton died unexpectedly in February that year, Van Buren was suddenly without a rival for political power in New York. On the national stage, however, tensions between the Northerners and Southerners brew. Van Buren deftly introduced a tariff that would help spread economic benefits to various groups, indicating that his camp was capable of effective legislation.

Van Buren eventually decided to return to New York to run for governor as the presidential election drew closer. This way, he could ensure that his state would support Jackson, who could then boost his reputation as an electable successor. As he campaigned across the various counties in his home state, voters could hardly fail to notice his elaborate and vividly colored attire:

"His complexion was bright blond and he dressed accordingly. On this occasion he wore an elegant snuff-colored broadcloth coat, with velvet collar to match; his cravat was orange tinted silk with modest lace tips; his vest was of pearl hue; his trousers were white duck; his silk hose corresponded to his vest, his shoes were Morocco; his nicely fitting gloves were yellow kid; his hat, a long-furred beaver, with broad brim, was of Quaker color[xxxi]."

With the help of alcohol, parades, speeches, and souvenirs, Van Buren secured a double victory. Jackson was elected as the Union's seventh president, and Van Buren secured the governorship by a large margin. Van Buren may have been envisioning his own presidency at the time, but his inaugural address as governor of New York indicated that he was also keenly aware of the new problems that the sprawling city was facing: the need for election reform, juvenile delinquency, and the need for bank regulation. He did not have many opportunities to address these issues, however, as Jackson soon offered him the position of secretary of state.

The position would place Van Buren back in Washington as Jackson's trusted right-hand man. Van Buren could not afford to miss this opportunity, as there was another rival for the presidency after Jackson's term was up. John Calhoun[xxxii], a South Carolina politician, had established the remarkable feat of becoming a vice president under two different presidencies (the Adams and Jackson presidencies). Like Van Buren, he had helped Jackson rise to power. The Washington political elites that were loyal to Jackson were soon split into two camps: those that favored Calhoun, and those that favored Van Buren.

As twenty thousand people arrived in Washington to ecstatically celebrate Jackson's inauguration in March 1829, Van Buren quietly acknowledged the dawn of a new era in his private notebook:

"Those who have wrought great changes in the world never succeeded by gaining over chiefs; but always by exciting the multitude. The first is the resource of intrigue and produces only secondary results, the second is the resort of genius and transforms the universe.[xxxiii]"

Chapter 5 – Secretary of State; Vice President In-Waiting

Andrew Jackson was the oldest man to become president at that point. At sixty-one, he had lived through the American Revolution himself, with a few battle scars as souvenirs. Despite his personal differences from Van Buren, both men would establish a productive working relationship and close personal ties throughout Jackson's two presidential terms.

Jackson's personal loyalties were certainly important to Van Buren's political prospects, as he had many enemies and opponents in Washington by this time. The newly formed Democratic Party was split into the Western politicians that Jackson had attracted, the Southerners who supported Calhoun, and Van Buren's clique of old-school Jeffersonians. Van Buren faced a particularly formidable foe in Calhoun, as he had personally ruined the South Carolinian's chance of competing for the presidency in 1824.

After all that campaigning, the task was now to govern the Union properly. To the envy and ire of his enemies, Van Buren became increasingly close to Jackson. Despite their different geographic origins, age difference, and temperament, the two men had their similarities and a number of complementary qualities. Jackson was prone to rage, a characteristic that Van Buren was able to deflect with his conciliatory nature and good sense of humor. Jackson had little patience for all the intrigue and gossip that haunted everything Van Buren did. Having just lost his wife Rachel, both men were widowers in a town where political wives exerted a significant influence through gossip, slander, and innuendo.

As we shall see, political alliances can be sealed by personal acts, rather than mere professionalism. It was Van Buren's personal conduct during the Peggy Eaton[xxxiv] affair (also known as the Petticoat Affair) that secured him Jackson's undying support, rather than how he executed his responsibilities as secretary of state. Peggy Eaton had arrived in Washington as the wife of John Eaton, secretary of war and Jackson's close friend. She was one of the unlikeliest women to become a Washington political wife, having been (1) the daughter of an innkeeper and (2) known for a history of sexual indiscretion – she had been in an adulterous relationship with Eaton when he was a Tennessee Senator and she was a married woman (they married after her husband died, with Jackson's approval).

Their marriage attracted major negative attention in the generally conservative Washington society. The other cabinet wives rallied around Calhoun's wife, Floride Bonneau Calhoun, in socially ostracizing Peggy. All of them ignored her whenever they met and refused to make social visits to the Eatons. Even Emily Donelson, the surrogate "First Lady" and niece of Andrew Jackson's late wife Rachel, sided with the Calhoun faction.

In *The Petticoat Affair: Manners, Mutiny, and Sex in Andrew Jackson's White House* (1997), John F. Marszalek explained why the women of Washington ("the petticoats") refused to accept Peggy:

"She did not know her place; she forthrightly spoke up about anything that came to her mind, even topics of which women were supposed to be ignorant. She thrust herself into the world in a manner inappropriate for a woman... Accept her, and society was in danger of disruption. Accept this uncouth, impure, forward, worldly woman, and the wall of virtue and morality would be breached and society would have no further defenses against the forces of frightening change. Margaret Eaton was not that important in herself; it was what she represented that constituted the threat. Proper women had no choice; they had to prevent her acceptance into society as part of their defense of that society's morality[xxxv]."

To understand why Jackson was so enraged by these developments, one must turn to his complicated marriage with Rachel Jackson[xxxvi]. Rachel Jackson was a pious woman who had *technically* converted adultery, and was subjected to malicious slander and opposition during Jackson's presidential campaign. They had been married in 1791, after she believed that her first husband (who she had abandoned for his violent behavior) had formally divorced her. She thus married Jackson again in 1794, after her husband finally divorced her in September 1793. When she died of a heart attack three months before Jackson's inauguration, he believed that this had been partly caused by the all of the negative publicity.

During this time, Van Buren stood apart by being personally friendly with Peggy. Was it their shared personal history as the children of humble tavern keepers? There was also the fact that Van Buren had no wife to influence him against her? One does not know if the friendship was a calculated move to win Jackson's favor, but it certainly placed him at odds with the prevailing moral opinion on Peggy Eaton. In any case, the scandal led Calhoun to fall out of personal favor with Jackson, while Van Buren was privately designated as his successor in an emergency by as early as December 1829.

Of course, Van Buren's ability to win favor with Jackson was also aided by his solid performance as an administrator of the State Department. His smooth-talking skills helped him excel as a diplomat, allowing him to obtain reciprocal trade benefits from the United Kingdom in the West Indies and to arrange for a large payment of 25 million francs from France (war debts that hailed back to Napoleon). Van Buren also arranged the first treaty with the Ottoman Empire, setting the foundation for American-Turkey relations that persist up to this day.

With Van Buren's aid, Jackson clarified the extent to which the federal government should support internal improvements in any individual state. Construction projects that benefited the Union as a whole - such as the constructions of ports, harbors, railway lines, or interstate roads – could be paid for with Federal funds. Projects that only benefited one particular state, however, should be funded with local state funds. This dictum may appear commonsensical now, but it was an important clarification during its time.

Meanwhile, Calhoun's opposition to Jackson, Van Buren, and their supporters had created a volatile political environment. Van Buren decided to diffuse the atmosphere by offering to resign – this would allow Jackson to invite other cabinet members such as John Eaton and a few of Calhoun's supporters to resign as well. Jackson eventually agreed with the idea, and had Van Buren be elected as minister to England.

On August 16, 1831, Van Buren sailed happily for England and escaped the never-ending political infighting in Washington. With his generous salary and all the hospitality he received, he was in the best of spirits. He met Washington Irving while socializing in London; Irving was then working as secretary to the American legation and was happy to take Van Buren and his eldest son sightseeing and drinking.

After a few months, Van Buren learned that the Senate had rejected his appointment as minister to England. Calhoun and his opponents had collectively cast the deciding vote against him, but their move to "kill him dead" eventually backfired. Van Buren gained national sympathy, as observers and journalists immediately concluded that the move had been politically motivated. He thus returned home as a martyr, at the precise moment when Jackson was looking for a new vice president.

When Van Buren returned to Washington, Jackson was embroiled in a conflict with the Bank of the United States. The bank was attempting to renew its charter and introduce a new tariff via Congress, which Jackson saw as an attempt to concentrate more wealth and power in the hands of the elite. Jackson famously vetoed the bill, creating more tension between the Northern and Southern members of the Union. A new party had sprung into existence with the main purpose of defeating Jackson and Van Buren: The Whigs.

During this episode – and a subsequent episode of conflict with Calhoun, who threatened to have South Carolina secede from the Union – Van Buren demonstrated that he could find a middle ground between the polarities of the North and South. When Jackson easily won a second term as president in 1832, Van Buren was his surefire pick as vice president – thus returning to preside over the Senate that had once rejected him.

Two years later, when the question of who would replace Jackson loomed all over Washington, Van Buren had to face a large number of rivals, enemies, and skeptics. Jackson's vocal support, however, was powerful and influential enough to secure him the Democratic nomination in May 1835. At only fifty-three, he became the youngest president to be elected at his time.

Chapter 6 –The Panic of 1837

At the dawn of his presidency in 1837, Van Buren was most probably in an optimistic frame of mind. He had just become the first president from New York, while New York City and his home state appeared to be destined for even more growth and greatness. He had prevailed against his political enemies and the wealthy elites that had underestimated him nearly every step of the way. He might have been looking forward to two solid presidential terms like his predecessor and staunch supporter Andrew Jackson.

At his inaugural address, Van Buren noted his relative youth (compared to previous presidents) and hailed the rise of a new generation to lead America. It had been half a century since the Constitution was proclaimed, and he used the opportunity to champion the grand experiment of American democracy. He also dared to mention the polarizing problem of slavery (this was the first time it had been addressed in an inaugural speech) but only promised that he would not interfere with it.

Reality, however, had other plans for the young president. Across the Atlantic, his British (monarchical) counterpart Queen Victoria[xxxvii] ascended to the throne in that same year. She would spend a longer time on the throne than any other British monarch; Van Buren would be forced to leave the White House after four years.

He did not have to wait long for signs of trouble. Thirteen days after Van Buren took control of the Oval Office, he learned that an economic crisis was at hand. If he had been paying closer attention the previous month, he would have noticed that the high price of flour had led to protests and the destruction of stores and warehouses in New York. As inflation ran amok and major banks started to close, the mobs grew in size and desperation. The great American experiment had hit its first major economic hurdle. By May 12, an unprecedentedly pessimistic view of the future had taken hold of the national psyche:

"The commercial distress and financial embarrassment pervade the whole nation. Posterity may get out of it, but the sun of the present generation will never again shine out. Things will grow better gradually, from the curtailment of business, but the glory has departed. Jackson, Van Buren and Benton form a triumvirate more fatal to the prosperity of America than Caesar, Pompey and Crassus were to the liberties of Rome[xxxviii]."

This pessimism spread to other American cities such as Baltimore, New Orleans, and Philadelphia – and to the other financial centers of Europe. If Van Buren did nothing to regain public confidence, there was a great risk that he would be thrown out of office in no time. He called an urgent Congress session on May 15 to diagnose the underlying causes of the Panic of 1837: the worst economic depression the nation had suffered thus far.

New York City's rise as a dominant commercial city – second only to London – had coincided with untrammeled growth and speculation across the nation. A large amount of the new wealth that was created had been generated by conventional means (iron, textiles, leather, steel, shipbuilding), but economic growth had also been fueled by the construction of a widespread railway network and the introduction of new fashions, toys, publications, and other novelty inventions. A voracious appetite for consumer goods had taken hold of the nation, matched by a disconcerting ability for bankers and speculators to make large amounts of money through a series of paper transactions.

To curb irresponsible speculation, Andrew Jackson had introduced the Specie Circular in 1836[xxxix]. This executive order mandated that any transaction involving public lands must be made in gold or silver. The aim was to rein in land speculation and reduce the amount of paper money in circulation. Jackson had also attempted to reduce the power of the Bank of the United States by reallocating federal funds to smaller state banks. These state banks nevertheless pursued high-risk credit policies that contributed to further speculation[xl] involving Western lands.

Van Buren thus inherited a difficult economic problem. The country's financial industry was overly regulated in some respects, while completely unregulated in other domains. There was no clear consensus on how much control the Federal government should extend over private banks. The American economy also suffered from a worsening balance of trade with England, foreign troubles in Ireland and England that motivated creditors to demand repayment, a fall in the price of cotton, and other crop failures.

The eighth president had been caught in a near-perfect storm. With high inflation and limited credit in circulation, economic activity was stifled across the nation. There was massive unemployment and a surge in the number of bankruptcies. Many died of starvation while others turn to begging as a means of surviving. The ports were lined with ships with nowhere to go, no goods to deliver, and no livelihoods to support.

As a loyal Jackson supporter, Van Buren was blamed by association. His political opponents made matters worse by arguing that his administration had been ineffective and complacent in alleviating the crisis. He was also in an ideological bind, as the Jeffersonian ideal of a constrained Federal government left him without the power and institutional apparatus to restore credit and remedy the nation's economic plight. He had to find a balance between the Jacksonians who insisted that the Federal government should keep its distance from the financial world, and those who wanted it to introduce more paper money into circulation.

On September 5, Van Buren called for a Panic session. He had devised a compromise that would please both sides. The Jacksonians were happy to hear that there would be an independent Treasury responsible for federal deposits, which would be separate from the nation's many private banks. Meanwhile, more Treasury notes would be printed and federal lawsuits against those who had reneged on payments would be delayed.

His proposal for an independent Treasury was nevertheless too radical for the House (it was approved by a small majority in the Senate). Without Jackson's charisma and ability to inspire and unite a broad swath of the American public, Van Buren also found it difficult to combat the impression that the Democrats were responsible for the nation's severe economic woes. He could sense the opposition biting at his heels at every turn, even in his home state.

The Van Buren administration had faced a major setback, but the economic climate eventually improved. Prices rebounded by the spring of 1839, but a second smaller depression that fall sealed the perception that Van Buren was unable to repair the nation's flawed financial system. The Great Magician might have been a whiz when it came to the acquisition of presidential power, but he was unable to prove himself as a genius in wielding it. It would take multiple generations before Franklin Delano Roosevelt[xli], America's 32nd president, would rise to the challenge of implementing an effective system of checks and balances to rein in the nation's complex financial ecosystem.

During this time, Van Buren successfully attempted to boost public perception by founding the *United States Magazine and Democratic Review*. The influential monthly magazine combined Democratic political commentary with innovative fiction from rising literary stars such as Nathaniel Hawthorne[xlii] (who had gained national fame with the publication of *The Scarlet Letter* in 1850) and a young Walter Whitman (who would publish the lauded poetry collection *Leaves of Grass* as Walt Whitman[xliii] in 1855). By shifting the blame for the Panic of 1837 to the Bank of the United States, it helped redeem Van Buren's reputation among the Democratic-leaning voters.

While Van Buren was ultimately unable to resolve the financial crisis, his actions as president did establish a precedent for consideration of the struggles of the urban poor. Its timing would nevertheless prove deadly for public confidence in his leadership. Before he came into office, the atmosphere was of unbridled confidence. The association of this painful bubble burst with his presidency would be almost impossible to shake off – even if his personal actions did not directly cause it.

Chapter 7 – American Gothic

To gain a sense of 1830s America, one can turn to the literary works of the writers that rose to prominence during this time. The birth of the American Gothic fiction can be traced to the rising influence of Edgar Allan Poe[xliv], Nathaniel Hawthorne, and Washington Irving. Their preoccupations with madness, terror, horror, and the supernatural can be traced to a greater awareness of the dark side of the American Dream that became increasingly visible now that its idealistic national narrative had been punctured. This was a nation of democratic ideals, the promise of economic wealth, and technological progress, yes, but it was also a society built on slavery, the colonization of Native American ancestral lands and their subsequent genocide, an obsession with racial purity, a rising number of immigrants, and a sprawling and unwieldy geographical terrain.

During this time, slavery became the undisputed heart of all this darkness. The first public protest against slavery in the Union could be traced back all the way to 1670s Pennsylvania[xlv], but it was still not a matter of national prominence in the 1830s. American participation in the African Slave trade had been outlawed in 1808, with Vermont being the only state to have definitely banned slavery. In the other Northern states such as Connecticut, Rhode Island, Massachusetts, New Hampshire, and Pennsylvania, an ambiguous process of gradual abolition[xlvi] was in place.

While the general perception that the Southern states relied on slavery far more than their Northern counterparts is true, it is also true that slavery was still persistent in the North. There may have been measures to prevent the growth of slavery there, but there was also no concerted measure to eradicate it altogether at this time. The general consensus about the "slavery question" at this time was that it would eventually disappear (which ultimately did not happen).

In the South, however, the gap between reality and ideals was impossible to ignore. There was a white class of privileged landowners who profited from the backbreaking labor of a black underclass without access to political power or information. With Van Buren in power as a Northern president, there was a general expectation that he would be less tolerant of slavery than his Southern predecessor.

It is difficult to sum up Van Buren's stance on slavery definitively. He may have been from the North, but he had worked hard to cultivate political alliances with the South throughout his career. He systematically managed to absent himself from divisive slavery votes, while making no mention of the issue in his private papers. His father had owned slaves, and so did he – unlike his Northern predecessors John Adams[xlvii] and John Quincy Adams (who were both from Massachusetts). If he had any deep sympathies for the anti-slavery movement, it did not stop him from attempting to suppress the New York abolitionist movement in the mid-1830s. He had supported the Gag Rules[xlviii] in 1836, which mandated that every abolitionist tract be tabled (i.e. that action be postponed) before they were read. Even so, some Southerners believed that he was a closet abolitionist who was hiding his sympathies for the sake of political gain.

As the nation became increasingly polarized, the middle ground that Van Buren had always held became more and more untenable. England had executed the 1833 Slavery Abolition Act – an ethical progress that Mexico had already achieved in 1838. The incompatibility of the ideal of American freedom and the persistence of American slavery could no longer be ignored during the Van

Buren presidency. Both sides of the debate would suffer death for their position. The Virginian revolt in 1831 had left fifty-five white Americans dead; Illinois abolitionist printer Elisha P. Lovejoy was murdered at his press in November 1837. By this time, New York alone was host to 274 abolition societies.

During this time, Van Buren was under unavoidable scrutiny by virtue of the greater political engagement he had engendered. The printing press meant that politicians could no longer tailor-make speeches for different constitutions, as whatever they said became printed and distributed across state and voting lines. Van Buren was under pressure from both sides to opt for a firm stance and risk alienating half of his support base either way. As a champion of democracy, he could not afford to sweep the debate under the carpet or place restrictions on anyone's freedom of speech.

In 1836, when Texas was declared an independent republic (it was previously a Mexican province) and aimed to join the Union, Van Buren was forced to make a definitive stance on slavery. Texas was a large slave-owning state; accepting it into the Union would enrage abolitionists in the North. Van Buren delayed his decision on the Texas question for months, which enraged both sides. Meanwhile, he was also criticized for extending Jackson's cruel legacy of removing Native Americans (the Cherokees and the Seminoles) from their tribal lands in the Southwest.

During the fall of 1837, both sides of the debates made their vociferous presence heard on Congress. Calhoun reemerged as slavery's passionate defender, arguing that it was intrinsic to the Southern way of life. He found a worthy opponent in former president John Quincy Adams, who denounced slavery with an equal ardor. These debates escalated to a bloody duel between two Congress Representatives: Jonathan Cilley (Maine) and William Graves (Kentucky). Cilley was killed, which led to a period of mourning among Washington society.

Van Buren's own slave had run away by this point in time, but his vice president, Kentucky's Richard Mentor Johnson[xlix] was personally inextricable from the institution of slavery. Johnson had fallen in love and married Julia Chinn, a mulatto that he had inherited from his father. Sexual relations between white masters and female slaves were commonplace, but Johnson pushed societal norms by treating Julia and their two daughters as family members. They traveled publicly together and attended dinners with guests. Johnson tried to get local society to accept them but unfortunately failed. Van Buren's Southern political allies (including Andrew Jackson) had attempted to have him removed from the vice presidency, but Van Buren had resisted their demands. When Johnson died in 1850, his own brothers made local court officials issue a document that claimed him to be childless and heirless.

There had been instances in the past where Van Buren's support for slave rights had enraged the South. In 1840, for example, a North Carolina naval court-martial case arrived at a legal roadblock: some of the witnesses were black, making their testimony illegal there. Van Buren had decided to defend their right to testify in this case. In other instances, however, Van Buren acted against slave interests since he could not afford to alienate his Southern support base.

His decision in 1839 has been immortalized by *Amistad*[l], the 1997 historical drama film directed by Steven Spielberg (he was portrayed by the English actor Nigel Hawthorne). That year, the slaves aboard the slave ship *La Amistad* mutinied and took over the ship. Two Spanish navigators were kept alive and instructed to take them back to Cuba, but they were directed towards Long Island instead. The American naval guard then arrested them. Their trial caught the attention of the abolitionist movement, including ex-president John Quincy Adams (who was seventy-three when he defended them in the Supreme Court). Adams eventually secured their freedom, while Van Buren was deemed the moral villain for demanding that the slaves be returned to their Spanish owners. (This is how he is characterized in the Spielberg film, which does not acknowledge the delicate middle ground Van Buren occupied with regard to slave rights).

Chapter 8 – Triumphs and Defeat

The Van Buren presidency was inevitably marred by the Panic of 1837 and the national divisions over slavery, but he also had reasons for celebration. As he proudly proclaimed during his inaugural address, his election as America's youngest president and the first to be born an American heralded the dawn of a new era: "I belong to a later age[li]." He was clearly Andrew Jackson's political successor, but it was also evident that his ascendancy to the Oval Office was a disruption in the status quo.

While he may not have been perceived or remembered as a moral hero, he certainly left his Washington peers with fond memories. He moved into the White House with four bachelor sons and no First Lady, but that position was not vacant for long. In 1838, his eldest son Abraham Van Buren married Angelica Singleton[lii], a young relative-by-marriage of Dolley Madison[liii] (James Madison's wife). Angelica became a renowned and enthusiastic hostess; the Southern belle from South Carolina would later be called the "Jackie Kennedy of the 19th century" for her renowned beauty and aristocratic manners.

Meanwhile, his son Martin, Jr. served as his principal secretary. Together, they would attend many lively dinner parties around Washington – where Van Buren would socialize amiably with Democrats and opposition party members alike. His consistent ability to separate his personal affiliations from his political leanings helped him gain favor with a wide range of local politicians and foreign diplomats. Despite his habit of fastidious dressing and his taste for fine food and furniture, Van Buren was happy to conduct himself with an air of informality and openness. He often attended official functions and public events without servants, attendants, or guards (or just one servant).

As a self-educated intellectual, Van Buren also created an environment where the intellectuals of his age could flourish. Apart from encouraging young writers and thinkers to publish in the *Democratic Review*, he also allocated jobs to historians and writers within his administration. America no longer needed to pay much attention to the intellectuals in Europe (as they had before); there were now local writers enthusiastically filling the pages of new magazines and newspapers, feeding the hunger for political information and commentary that Van Buren had encouraged.

It is thus not surprising that many new patent applications were filed during this era. As steamboats began to cut the time it took to cross the Atlantic in April 1838, the time it took to travel from London to New York reduced to only two weeks. Photography arrived in America soon after the camera was invented in France, giving the world the first photograph of the moon.

America's dawning potential as a champion of discovery and progress was also symbolized by the United States Exploring Expedition (U.S. Ex. Ex.), a scientific expedition to explore the Southern Hemisphere and hitherto unexplored corners of the Pacific Ocean. With Van Buren's personal interest and support, six vessels and 346 men sailed from Virginia in 1838 to circumnavigate the world. When they returned home as national and scientific heroes in 1842, they had traveled 87, 000 miles – including 1,500 miles of the Antarctic coastline.

Van Buren also helped the country steer away from costly conflicts with Great Britain. Tensions were still high when the Canadian rebellion against then-reigning world power erupted in the fall of 1837, close to the New York border. Many New Yorkers were eager to support the movement against their old enemy, leading to one American casualty and the risk of an open confrontation. Since the American army was already occupied with battling the Seminoles in Florida, he could ill-afford armed conflict with the British. He effectively managed to keep the conflict under control during this time.

When another conflict occurred along the northeast border between Maine and Canada a year later, Van Buren's diplomatic skills were put to good use once again. This time, the problem was caused by the fact that the border had never been settled properly – leading to both sides accusing the other of being trespassers. With the help of General Winfield Scott (once again), discussions in Washington prevented the conflict from escalating.

There are two other Van Buren claims to fame that many may not associate with his name. On March 31, 1840, he extended the urban poor a helping hand by issuing an executive order that decreed a ten-hour day for all federal workers. This was a major step in protecting worker rights, especially at a time when many were expected to work from dawn to dusk.

His other influence was in mainstream language. In the spring of 1839, Bostonians began to use the phrase "OK" to replace "oil correct" – a common slang for saying "all right." The phrase OK had also been used by Van Buren supporters as an acronym for "Old Kinderhook" (which was possibly inspired by Jackson's nickname, "Old Hickory"). Van Buren even began to write "OK" next to his official signatures. The rest, as they say, is history. It became wildly popular and resonated as an expression of American optimism, informality and efficiency – and is now used all over the world nearly two centuries later.

Van Buren's social, symbolic, and intellectual triumphs during his presidency would nevertheless prove insufficient to secure his reelection in 1841. He had his supporters, but by this time he also had a wide range of enemies. Van Buren became the target of Andrew Jackson's opponents, those who were critical of the federal government, and those who loathed any form of government intervention in the economy. The Southerners suspected him of being a closet abolitionist, while the Northerners were suspicious of his alliance with Southern politics. Even he perceived that all his diplomacy and amiability could do little to dull their antagonism: "Why the deuce is it that they have such an itch for abusing me? I tried to be harmless, and positively good-natured, & a most decided friend of peace[liv]."

In Van Buren's first job as a legal apprentice, his country bumpkin appearance was deemed to be a major problem. At this juncture in his life, his sophisticated taste would be used against him. During the campaign season leading up to the 1841, a Whig representative from Pennsylvania effectively tainted Van Buren's reputation by painstakingly going through the list of expenditures that had been incurred via his attempt to introduce some European sophistication to the White House. By taking note of all the trees, furniture, shrubbery, and landscaping that was involved, Charles Ogle painted Van Buren in an impossibly aristocratic and extravagant light. In the context of the worst economic crisis the nation had faced, the mention of exotic plants, exquisite French furniture, and costly renovations placed Van Buren in an extremely unfavorable light.

The Whigs used every opportunity to tarnish Van Buren's legacy and presented their own candidate – William Henry Harrison[lv], a senior military hero – as the antithesis of Van Buren's corrupt and insensitive decadence. Harrison had actually grown up in a brick mansion in Virginia, but the public imagination was captured by the rumor that he had an impoverished childhood and lived in a log cabin. Despite originating from an aristocratic Virginian family, he was a man of the people, a man of "hard cider and a log cabin." Van Buren's humble origins were made invisible by his depiction as a champagne-swirling fop and dandy, dining with silver spoons in the

White House. By this time, the Whigs had mastered the sophisticated political tactics that Van Buren had developed, and were keen to grasp as much political power as possible from the Democrats.

Van Buren's decision to nominate Richard Johnson as his vice president during his reelection campaign also created some internal divisions within the Democratic Party. They tried to champion him as a defender of democracy, and "the pilot that weathered the storm!" but these slogans were less catchy than all the anti-Van Buren songs that proliferated during this time. They had lyrics like ""Van, Van, he's a used up man" and "Old Tip he wears a homespun coat / He has no ruffled shirt-wirt-wirt / But Mat he has the golden plate / And he's a little squirt-wirt-wirt." There was also a ditty which uncharacteristically presented him in an unholy light:

"Who rules us with an iron rod?

Who rules at Satan's beck and call?

Who heeds not man? Who heeds not God?

Van Buren![lvi]"

He did his best to recapture public approval, but his efforts on the campaign trail were not enough to turn the tide around. When the results were announced, he learned that he had won only six states (out of the 26 states that had joined the Union by then). He prevailed in South Carolina, Virginia, Illinois, New Hampshire, Alabama and Arkansas – but lost his home state of New York. He was arguably the first president to have lost a re-election campaign due to a savvy public relations campaign. William Henry Harrison secured an overwhelming victory, capturing 80 percent of ballots cast by the voting population (who were then all white men). The Whigs also won the House of Congress, leaving the Democratic Party at a severe disadvantage.

Ex-president John Quincy Adams may have been happy to see Van Buren defeated, but he was dismayed with how the victory was won.

The political campaigns that unfolded in the lead-up to the election were filled with cheap political slogans and an obvious lack of sportsmanship between the two competing parties. Many wondered if this was a signal that the ideal of democracy had been corrupted.

Van Buren's political career had ended prematurely, but his spirits had not been crushed. Despite the severe defeat, he calmly summed up his administrations successes and failures during his last speech to Congress. He acknowledged that the banks had failed to perform their duties, while noting that foreign relations had flourished. He also took the opportunity to remedy accusations of extravagance by duly noting that expenditures for ordinary purposes had been significantly reduced during his time in office.

After attending William Henry Harrison's damp inaugural ceremony, he headed north – back to the home state he had been away from for two decades. When his ship arrived at the Manhattan port, he was heartened by the homecoming welcome he received. Despite the heavy rain, a larger number of the city's poor stood waiting for him – eager to greet the man who had represented their interests in a political establishment where they had very few allies. A Whig opponent (George Templeton Strong) described the scene while expressing his disapproval of it:

"Had to wait half an hour in the drizzle at the corner of Rector Street and Broadway while Matty's triumphal procession was going up. A disgusting assemblage of the unwashed democracy they were, generally speaking, a more rowdy, draggle-tailed, jailbird-resembling gang of truculent loafers than the majority of them I never witnessed before. Considering the rain, they turned out in force—and the rain, by the by, was a blessing to some of them, for the ablution was badly needed. Butler boys on horseback—there was an unlimited number of them. Carts with twenty little blackguards sticking to each, a dozen grand marshals with chapeaux and swords galloping about and getting into everybody's way in the intensity of their excitement, several very formidable brass bands, divers gorgeous banners, and so forth, with a great predominance of pedestrians from the neighborhood of the Points apparently, passed one; and then came the triumphal car, to wit, a shabby barouche and four with Matty himself, hat in hand, looking as happy as a man could be expected to in the rain without hat or umbrella. He looks older than I supposed[lvii]."

Chapter 9 – Comebacks

After spending two weeks in Manhattan (where he made many public appearances), Van Buren made his way up to Hudson River to Kinderhook. The small community of Dutch farmers erupted into chaos when he arrived there on May 8, 1841. A large portion of the community assembled at the steamboat wharf to welcome their most famous resident home. Van Buren was greeted by a firing artillery piece, a brass band, a carriage, firing cannons, bells, and many long-winded speeches. When it was his turn to address the crowd, Van Buren thanked them for their enthusiastic welcome and claimed that he did not regret his fiscal policies or the political path he had undertaken. The ceremonies of the day ended on a jubilant and optimistic note when his old friend Benjamin Butler reminded the crowd of all the obstacles that Van Buren had overcome on his journey from that very small town to the White House.

Van Buren then made his way to Lindenwald, the large mansion on the outskirts of Kinderhook that he had thoughtfully purchased in 1839 – in the event that he would not be able to live in the White House for another presidential term. The house had once belonged to the Van Ness family that had attempted to thwart Van Buren's rise. Once there, he began to undertake ambitious renovation plans. The house had been built in 1797 as a two and one-half story red brick Georgian-style house. He eliminated the stairway, and installed fashionable French scenic wallpaper in the center hall with the intention of using it for balls and banquets[lviii]. More extensive renovations would be completed in 1849, involving the addition of modern amenities (running water, a bathroom, kitchen ranges, and a furnace which was one of the first central heating systems in the Hudson Valley). With a four-story brick tower, attic dormers, a new front porch, a central gable, a yellow coat of paint, it effectively became a flashy Italian villa.

In his splendid isolation, Van Buren plotted his next political steps. He was only fifty-eight, and his political career was already seemingly over. After being in charge of the entire nation for four whole years, now all he had to contemplate was what crops to plant on his farm and when to plant them. Instead of being disheartened by the prospect of rural life, he astounded the local farmers with his ability to work on his farm himself. He worked the fields and built dams and orchards to improve the farmland (which would eventually increase to 191 acres out of the 225-acre estate after several land acquisitions). Van Buren still read voraciously, wrote letters, and spent ample amounts of money on entertaining his visitors. Three of his four sons lived nearby, and he welcomed a grandson into the world during his first summer on the farm.

As the presidential election of 1844 drew near, however, Van Buren contemplated the possibility of running another presidential campaign. Harrison had died a month after he entered office (due to pneumonia), and was replaced by his vice president John Tyler. Tyler was a former Democrat who was now distrusted by the Democrats and the Whigs. There was therefore a chance that he could reclaim what should have been his.

To kick things off, Van Buren embarked on an ambitious campaign trail. From Kinderhook, he headed south – to Philadelphia, Baltimore, Charleston, Georgia, Alabama, Mississippi and New Orleans. He then made his way up the Mississippi River to Memphis, and across Tennessee to visit Andrew Jackson at The Hermitage. After the reunion, he went through Kentucky to arrive at the emerging city of Chicago. During a layover in the small town of Rochester, Illinois, a stroke of luck allowed Van Buren to meet a young Abraham Lincoln[lix]. Van Buren was impressed and amused by all of Lincoln's stories, without any inkling that he might have made a significant impression on the future 16th president of the United States.

When he returned home to Lindenwald in July 1842, Van Buren had crossed over seven thousand miles and shook hands with over 200,000 people. His reentry into political life had been reenergizing; articles demanding his return to national politics were soon published, circulated, read and discussed.

He began to clarify his position towards slavery at this point in time. His time in the Northwest had aligned him more closely with the abolitionist movement, and he began to become more impatient with the South for refusing to change with the times. The question of whether Texas was to enter the Union had become a pressing issue once more, and each political candidate running for office needed to have a clear position – and the risk of alienating either the Northern or Southern voting bloc. The entry of Texas was not only contentious because it would reintroduce slavery. Its large size would also recalibrate the balance of power between the North and the South.

Andrew Jackson had voiced his support behind Texas's entry into the Union, and Van Buren was expected to support his old mentor. Instead, Van Buren shocked observers by stating, in no uncertain terms, that he opposed the Texas annexation. He argued that the desire for more real estate would stifle American's pursuit of "reason and justice", and would also risk war with Mexico. Van Buren had defied all the critics who had accused him of being spineless and lacking strong principles, but he also angered key allies in Virginia, Pennsylvania, and the other Southern strongholds.

His supporters knew that Van Buren's presidential bid was an uncertain proposition, but they expected him to secure the Democratic nomination. Instead, they were thwarted by the anachronistic requirement that he secure the votes of two-thirds of the delegates to the Democratic National Convention (this rule would be removed in 1936, by Franklin D. Roosevelt). Van Buren had the majority of the votes, but he fell short on this requirement because the neutral delegates had been bought off with dishonest promises. Initially the clear winner, other newcomers who had a softer stance towards slavery and Texas began to prevail. Tennessee's James Polk[lx] eventually emerged as the first "dark horse" candidate in the history of the presidency.

The party he helped create had thus abandoned Van Buren. He did not give up hope on the Democrats, however. He focused his energies on ensuring that New York voters swung to support the relatively unknown Polk, with the hopes that his efforts would be rewarded appropriately when Polk had to select his new cabinet. Polk ultimately won, defeating his Whig rival Henry Clay[lxi] and taunts such as "Who is James. K. Polk?" When he was announced the 11th president of the United States, he opted to ignore all of Van Buren's recommendations and installed a rival New York clique in prominent positions instead.

If he had once felt that he was taking to politics like a fish to water, that was no longer the case. During his presidency, Polk waged a war against Mexico (the Mexican War[lxii], 1846 – 1848) and secured large swaths of new territory for the nation. The divisions between the pro-slavery and the anti-slavery camps (then nicknamed Hunkers and Barnburners) became more severe. The Democratic ideals that Van Buren had hailed during his inaugural presidential speech were difficult to find in 1845. The party he had helped to build over the past few decades was now being torn apart. He had been personally betrayed and humiliated, and his old mentor Andrew Jackson had just passed away.

In early 1848, Van Buren retreated to a hotel in Washington Square, New York, to take stock of the political status quo. There, he wrote his "Barnburner Manifesto", which insisted that the national party grant the Barnburners recognition as the true representatives of New York Democracy. He also argued that it should impose a ban on slavery on all the new territory that Polk had acquired from Mexico. By drawing from the ideas outlined by the Founding Fathers[lxiii], Van Buren effectively used his reputation as an ex-president to argue that the persistence and expansion slavery had never been a part of the American mythology.

Upon publication, Van Buren's manifesto drew a large amount of attention in New York. His son, John Van Buren, who was now actively involved in politics, asked him to run for the presidency again – this time as a candidate of the new party he was establishing. The climate at the time was certainly ripe for the birth of a new party. The Revolutions of 1848[lxiv] had captured the American imagination with the renewed promise of democracy as European monarchies in Sicily, France, Germany, Italy and Austria were overthrown. The California Gold Rush[lxv] had begun just as the Mexican War was coming to an end. Abraham Lincoln – then an unknown first-term Illinois congressman - embodied the strange behavior of politicians at the time by brazenly opposing Polk's aggression against the Mexicans and alienating a large segment of his voting base.

When the Barnburners failed to secure the Democratic nomination during the national Democratic convention that May, the stage was set for them to switch allegiances to the new party. Van Buren was asked to run for the presidency one more time, and he rose to the occasion with an unprecedentedly vocal and overt opposition towards slavery. He argued that Congress should not be neutral towards the vexing issue, but should instead use its power to prevent it from spreading any further.

On August 9, the Barnburners organized a Buffalo gathering that attracted twenty thousand people. The Free Soil campaign was born, attracting Northern Democrats and Whigs to support a mixed bag ideology that included an opposition to slavery and an emphasis on economic opportunity for all ("Free Soil, Free Speech, Free Labor, and Free Men!"). As the presidential nominee, Van Buren openly attacked the Slave Power movement with Charles Francis Adams (the son of John Quincy Adams) as the vice presidential nominee. The news of Van Buren's curious new political position elicited mixed responses. Some denounced him as a "fallen man", a "traitor", and a "hypocrite", while others lauded his transition towards a more liberal position in older age (a rarity among most politicians).

When the electoral votes were tallied, he learned that he had garnered an impressive 291,804 votes in total (10% of the total). Unfortunately, he had failed to win any state. The Whig candidate Zachary Taylor[lxvi] prevailed over Democrat Lewis Cass by securing 165 electoral votes and 1.36 million popular votes. The Free Soil movement had been defeated, but it nevertheless made history by being the country's first major third-party bid for the presidency. It also served to remind the Democratic Party that it could not remain pro-slavery if it wished to retain its support base.

Van Buren's unexpected defection from the Democratic Party was ill-advised from the standpoint of political strategy, but it was a moral victory nonetheless. He had unambiguously decried slavery in public, and his actions had matched his principles even when it was not politically expedient.

Chapter 10 – Retirement

After his third bid for the presidency failed, Van Buren finally accepted the prospect of a permanent retirement from politics. The number of visitors to Lindenwald would slowly decrease as the years passed by, leaving more time for Van Buren to spend with his family and friends. Being permanently removed from Washington must have been difficult for the professional politician, but there was also some comfort in being apart from the increasingly divisive political climate of the 1850s. There was no hope for any reconciliation between the North and South by this time.

Despite being accused of indulging in too much fine cuisine and wine, his health was in good shape. He had outlived so many of his contemporaries and rivals. Apart from Andrew Jackson and John Quincy Adams, Van Buren would outlive Polk (who passed on in 1849), Zachary Taylor (1850), Calhoun (1850), Clay (1852) and Webster (1852). He was now the oldest ex-president, presiding over a political scene filled with younger people that were relatively unfamiliar with his legacy.

Without a country to run or a political campaign to plan, Van Buren devoted his energies to upgrading his massive estate. With great shock and ceremony, he introduced the then-unprecedented concept of the indoor toilet. He still kept abreast of political developments with the aid of newspapers and informants. In 1850, he finally realigned himself with the Democratic Party even though it still hosted many pro-slavery members. After his overt opposition to slavery during the Free Soil campaign, he reverted to a more moderate position that opposed it in principle without championing its immediate eradication: "I have nothing to modify or change. The end of slavery will come—amid terrible convulsion, I fear, but it will come[lxvii]."

Instead of being looked after by his sons in his later years, he still had to play the role of caregiver. His fourth son, Smith Thomas Van Buren, was preparing to be a widower with three children as his wife slowly died of consumption. His third son Martin Van Buren Jr. suffered from ill health and had to endure long and trying journeys to access the expertise of distant doctors. His second son, John Van Buren, never realized the early political promise he had demonstrated. He had been suggested as a vice presidential candidate in 1852, but his affinity for nightlife had cost him his support base. (His eldest son Abraham Van Buren was nevertheless in good health – he helped to publish his father's presidential papers and served as the chief defender of his presidential legacy).

Van Buren was still a symbol of strength and longevity, but he knew that death would eventually claim him, as it had claimed all of his political heroes and mentors. With the help of Thomas Hart Benson, an old friend and an ex-Missouri senator, he began to immortalize his life story by writing *Thirty Years' View* – an ambitious political memoir that arguably pioneered the genre in America. He also helped John Hamilton craft a biography of his famed father Alexander Hamilton, and served as a sagely older figure to those who wished to obtain a firsthand view of what it was like to stand in the presence of the nation's Founding Fathers.

Did Van Buren look for love in his later years, after decades of being a widower and avoiding the taint of a scandal? There are no records to conclusively prove this, but the town records reveal that he spent a fair amount of time visiting the grave of an unknown woman, located in a private burial plot three miles away from the village: "Some of us know of one of Kinderhook's estimable and cultivated women who declined to marry the ex-President[lxviii]." The most probable speculation of her identity: Margaret Silvester, the spinster daughter of Francis Silvester (the local lawyer who gave him his very first job[lxix]).

Van Buren's memoir, being as ambitious as it was, took years to finish. He began writing it in 1854 while traveling around Europe with his ill son Martin. He meticulously wrote down all the political maneuvers he undertook over the decades, while also taking note of the history of political parties. His focus was uneven, but he ultimately ensured that many intriguing insights of life during his era were recorded for posterity.

He also tried to pass on his political wisdom to John Van Buren, misguidedly hoping that he stood a chance to assume control of the White House like he did. He tellingly warned him about the dangers of being perceived as a professional politician: "There is regard him as a wanton upon Providence, and are constantly disposed to show him the cold shoulder. Although many make their living by it, they get it by hook or crook, and no public honors sit well upon them[lxx]."

In 1858, Van Buren recovered from a severe fall from his galloping horse. Despite his attempts to prevent the Southern states from attempting to secede from the Union, the Civil War[lxxi] broke out on April 12, 1861. He may have cultivated many alliances with the South in the past, but he now stood firmly alongside Abraham Lincoln to insist that the battle be valiantly fought to preserve the integrity and ideals of the Union: "The attack upon our flag and the capture of Fort Sumter by the Secessionists could be regarded in no other light than as the commencement of a treasonable attempt to overthrow the Federal Government by military force[lxxii]."

As a newly elected president from the vehemently antislavery Republican Party, Lincoln certainly benefited from Van Buren's vocal support. The seven Southern States of South Carolina, Mississippi, Florida, Alabama, Georgia, Louisiana, and Texas had carried out their threat to secede soon after he was announced president, forcing his administration into crisis mode. Lincoln refused to accept the Confederate States of America as a sovereign entity; he deemed them to be rebelling states instead. 75,000 militiamen were recruited to battle for three months. The events during this time are arguably best captured by Stephen Crane's psychologically astute war novel *The Red Badge of Courage*[lxxiii] (1895).

What would turn out to be the bloodiest war in the history of the United States inevitably took its toll on Van Buren's health. After years of good health, he began to be consumed by illness. He passed away on July 24, 1862, slightly over a year after the war had begun. Despite the ongoing battle against the Confederate troops[lxxiv], Lincoln made sure that the entire nation mourned his departure:

"The President with deep regret announces to the people of the United States the decease, at Kinderhook, N.Y., on the 24th Instant, of his honored predecessor Martin Van Buren.

This event will occasion mourning in the nation for the loss of a citizen and a public servant whose memory will be gratefully cherished. Although it has occurred at a time when his country is afflicted with division and civil war, the grief of his patriotic friends will measurably be assuaged by the consciousness that while suffering with disease and seeing his end approaching his prayers were for the restoration of the authority of the Government of which he had been the head and for peace and good will among his fellow-citizens[lxxv]."

During the next six months, all U. S. Army and Navy officers wore black crape on their left arms as they engaged in some of the deadliest fighting during the four-year war – as a tribute to the eighth president. Kinderhook staged the grandest event in its history to mourn the death of its most famous son, with thousands attending his funeral ceremony. His casket was accompanied by no less than eighty-one carriages and a long line of people from all walks of life

– politicians, clerics, and the common man – accompanying him to his final resting spot in Kinderhook Cemetery[lxxvi].

Three years later, Lincoln prevailed in his quest to ensure that the Union would not be divided. On January 31, 1865, Congress finally abolished slavery with the Thirteenth Amendment[lxxvii]. The Federal forces had suffered from 360,000 deaths by this time, while their opponents had lost 258,000 men. The war was estimated to have cost the nation over $15 billion.

Conclusion

Van Buren may have been a lively presence in the American public consciousness during his lifetime, but his legacy does not enjoy the same immortality as Lincoln or the Founding Fathers that preceded him. His books were published posthumously, starting with the *Inquiry into the Origin and Course of Political Parties in the United States* (1867) five years after his death. His lengthy memoir would take a staggering fifty-three years to enter the book market, since the *Autobiography of Martin Van Buren* was only published in 1920. By then, interest in this life and political legacy had died down.

The few existing biographies of Martin Van Buren reflect his status as one of America's lesser-known presidents. Van Buren had no grand claim to symbolic fame, and he left behind no defining policies that would keep his memory alive in the national consciousness. His unapologetic opposition to slavery only became known after he was no longer in the White House, and thus unable to influence key decisions that would affect the balance of power between the abolitionist movement and the slavery apologists. By then, it was too little, too late. Historians duly note his reputation as a skilled negotiator and diplomat who kept the United States out of war, but that it is not solely sufficient to capture the imaginations of future generations. A politician's refusal to compromise political success for the sake of ideological purity is, after all, the order of the day in most historical periods.

If Van Buren's attitudes towards slavery can still be defended, his continuation of Andrew Jackson's devastating plan for Indian removal is far less redeemable. The Trail of Tears[lxxviii] ultimately involved the forced relocation of 100,000 indigenous people from their homes in the Southeast region of the United States to the Indian territories that lay west of the Mississippi River. The Cherokee, Creek, Chickasaw, Choctaw, and Seminole tribes were made to abandon their ancestral land and walk across nine states and 5,045 miles (8,120 km) for the benefit of American settlers and land speculators. The Second Seminole War had begun in 1835, before Van Buren's presidency, and continued after he left office. His successor President Tyler eventually agreed to end the American Army's costliest Indian war in 1842, by allowing the surviving Seminoles (approximately 300 of them) to live in reservations in Florida (Van Buren had rejected these very same terms in 1838).

Despite his shortcomings, Van Buren inspired several notable poets and writers. Walt Whitman noted that he was a "brilliant manager" towards the end of his life. 20th-century modernist poet Ezra Pound[lxxix] would wax lyrical about his populist achievements in "Canto 37" in his *Seventy Cantos:*

""THOU shalt not," said Martin Van Buren, "jail 'em for debt.

That an immigrant should set out with good banknotes

and find 'em at the end of his voyage

but waster paper … if a man have in primeval forest

set up his cabin, shall rich patrons take it from him?

High judges? – are, I suppose, subject to passions

as have affected other great and good men, also

subject to *spirit de corps*[lxxx]. "

In his 1973 historical novel *Burr,* Gore Vidal[lxxxi] revived the speculation that Aaron Burr was actually Van Buren's biological father.

He also lived on in the memories of the younger politicians he had influenced during his lifetime. This included several of Lincoln's close supporters (Frank Blair, Montgomery Blair, Gideon Welles, and vice president Hannibal Hamlin). There was also Samuel Tilden, who would go on to become governor of New York and a Democratic presidential nominee in the 1876 election. Van Buren may not be recalled as a key figure in the history of the Democratic Party, but his impact on its legacy and structure is undeniable. Without Van Buren, the ideals of the free market, personal liberty, free trade, and reduced government intervention would not be at the core of the Democratic Party today.

We also tend to hold wartime presidents in a more favorable light, since they are given the opportunity to attain national heroism and stir up patriotic sentiments when the nation had to be bravely defended against foreign enemies or opposing ideals. Peacemaking presidents spare their country from the economic ravages of war and the heartbreaking score of casualties, but their efforts are often taken for granted. By paying closer attention to the nationalist bias that is often present in the historical record, we can better appreciate Van Buren's commitments towards peace, neutrality – as well as his diplomatic ability that allowed the United States to stay out of armed conflict with Mexico, Canada, and Britain during his presidency.

While Van Buren was not able to "magically" rescue the nation from the worst economic crisis it had ever experienced at that point in time, his logical and rational approach to the problem helped pave the way for future governments to react to similar problems. Historian Glyndon G. Van Deusen fairly summarizes Van Buren's performance in this capacity:

"With all his weaknesses, the fact remains that Van Buren was honest; that he knew the value of and habitually sought counsel; that he deliberated before making decisions; and that his four years in the White House demonstrated, for better or for worse, a perfectly logical development of the left-wing tendencies of Jacksonian Democracy, a development which it took courage to foster in the face of a catastrophic depression[lxxxii]."

After he died, Van Buren's cherished home of Lindenwald became a private residence, a tea house, and a nursing home as it fell into different hands over the years[lxxxiii]. It was purchased by the National Park Service in 1973, which then began to carefully restore it over the following decades, effectively reversing years of neglect. The wallpaper patterns, carpets, and furniture were painstakingly reproduced to accurately reflect the home as Van Buren had lived in it. In 1988, the Park Service opened the Martin Van Buren National Historic Site to the public.

Long after his death, the political battles that Van Buren fought remain no less pertinent. The interests of the common people still have to be defended against wealthy corporations and dynastic elites. Democratic ideals – the right for free speech, freedom of the press, and the right of the people to govern themselves – still need to be safeguarded against tyranny and authoritarianism. The name Van Buren may seem synonymous with the trappings of wealth and aristocracy, but it is always worth noting that the man himself was a tavern keeper's son who was not afraid to curtail the interest of the business elites throughout his political career. His political rise coincided with the wave of commercialism sweeping through antebellum American and New York's rise as a political and economic power (which displaced Virginia and the South) – but Van Buren took important measures to ensure that the common and underprivileged were not cannibalized and exploited during the process.

Since Van Buren's presidency is relatively unknown, it is easy to forget the specifics and mischaracterize it. For example, George Bush thanked him in his first news conference after becoming the 43rd president of the United States. Van Buren was cited for "paving the way" for him in terms of being the last incumbent Vice President to be elected President[lxxxiv]. What was not mentioned was the fact that Van Buren had been blamed for all the shortcomings of the Andrew Jackson presidency, while being unfavorably compared to the charismatic military hero.

His legacy may be marred by the Panic of 1837 and his waffling position on slavery, but his life trajectory itself reflects the (often unfulfilled) promise of the American dream. As a president, he ultimately stands among the other "not-quite-heroic" figures[lxxxv] that fade into the background when compared to the moral giants of American history – but that does not diminish the importance of the life lessons we can learn from examining his biography.

Primary and Secondary Sources

[i] "Martin Van Buren". *History.com*. **https://www.history.com/topics/us-presidents/martin-van-buren**. Accessed 10 March 2018.

[ii] "July 4th". *History.com*. **https://www.history.com/topics/holidays/july-4th**. Accessed 10 March 2018.

[iii] Widmer, Edward L. *Martin Van Buren: The American Presidents Series: The 8th President, 1837-1841*. 2003.

[iv] "Does the tallest presidential candidate win?" *Thought Catalog*. **https://www.thoughtco.com/does-the-tallest-presidential-candidate-win-3367512**. Accessed 10 March 2018.

[v] "Martin Van Buren". *Encyclopaedia Britannica*. **https://www.britannica.com/biography/Martin-Van-Buren**. Accessed 10 March 2018.

[vi] "Andrew Jackson". *History.com*. **https://www.history.com/topics/us-presidents/andrew-jackson**. Accessed 10 March 2018.

[vii] "Free-Soil Party". *Encyclopaedia Britannica*. **https://www.britannica.com/topic/Free-Soil-Party**. Accessed 10 March 2018.

[viii] "Albany". *Encyclopaedia Britannica*. **https://www.britannica.com/place/Albany-New-York**. Accessed 10 March 2018.

[ix] "Federalist Party". *Encyclopaedia Britannica.*
https://www.britannica.com/topic/Federalist-Party. Accessed 10 March 2018.

[x] "Thomas Jefferson". *Encyclopaedia Britannica.*
https://www.britannica.com/biography/Thomas-Jefferson. Accessed 10 March 2018.

[xi] "Washington Irving". *Encyclopaedia Britannica.*
https://www.britannica.com/biography/Washington-Irving. Accessed 10 March 2018.

[xii] "New York City in the 19th Century." *Thought Catalog.*
https://www.thoughtco.com/new-york-city-19th-century-1774031. Accessed 10 March 2018.

[xiii] "Aaron Burr". *Encyclopaedia Britannica.*
https://www.britannica.com/biography/Aaron-Burr. Accessed 10 March 2018.

[xiv] "Tammany Hall". *Encyclopaedia Britannica.*
https://www.britannica.com/topic/Tammany-Hall. Accessed 10 March 2018.

[xv] Fitzpatrick, John Clement, and Martin Van Buren. *The autobiography of Martin Van Buren*. 2011.

[xvi] "War of 1812". *Encyclopaedia Britannica.*
https://www.britannica.com/event/War-of-1812. Accessed 10 March 2018.

[xvii] Widmer, Edward L. *Martin Van Buren: The American Presidents Series: The 8th President, 1837-1841*. 2003.

[xviii] Ibid.

[xix] "Alexander Hamilton". *Encyclopaedia Britannica.*
https://www.britannica.com/biography/Alexander-Hamilton-United-States-statesman. Accessed 10 March 2018.

[xx] "DeWitt Clinton". *Encyclopaedia Britannica.*
https://www.britannica.com/biography/DeWitt-Clinton-American-politician. Accessed 10 March 2018.

[xxi] "Jeffersonianism". *Merriam-Webster.* **https://www.merriam-webster.com/dictionary/Jeffersonianism.** Accessed 10 March 2018.

[xxii] Widmer, Edward L. *Martin Van Buren: The American Presidents Series: The 8th President, 1837-1841.* 2003.

[xxiii] "Slavery in the United States". *Encyclopaedia Britannica.*
https://www.britannica.com/topic/slavery-in-the-United-States. Accessed 10 March 2018.

[xxiv] Ibid.

[xxv] Widmer, Edward L. *Martin Van Buren: The American Presidents Series: The 8th President, 1837-1841.* 2003.

[xxvi] "Constitution of the United States of America". *Encyclopaedia Britannica.*
https://www.britannica.com/topic/Constitution-of-the-United-States-of-America. Accessed 10 March 2018.

[xxvii] "John Quincy Adams". *Encyclopaedia Britannica.*
https://www.britannica.com/biography/John-Quincy-Adams. Accessed 10 March 2018.

[xxviii] "Erie Canal". *Encyclopaedia Britannica.*
https://www.britannica.com/topic/Erie-Canal. Accessed 10 March 2018.

[xxix] "Andrew Jackson". *Encyclopaedia Britannica.*
https://www.britannica.com/biography/Andrew-Jackson. Accessed 10 March 2018.

[xxx] Widmer, Edward L. *Martin Van Buren: The American Presidents Series: The 8th President, 1837-1841.* 2003.

[xxxi] Ibid.

[xxxii] "John C. Calhoun". *Encyclopaedia Britannica.*
https://www.britannica.com/biography/John-C-Calhoun. Accessed 10 March 2018.

xxxiii Widmer, Edward L. *Martin Van Buren: The American Presidents Series: The 8th President, 1837-1841.* 2003.

xxxiv "Margaret Eaton". *Encyclopaedia Britannica.* **https://www.britannica.com/biography/Margaret-Eaton**. Accessed 10 March 2018.

xxxv Marszalek, John F. *The Petticoat Affair: Manners, Mutiny, and Sex in Andrew Jackson's White House.* 1997.

xxxvi "Rachel Jackson". *Encyclopaedia Britannica.* **https://www.britannica.com/biography/Rachel-Jackson**. Accessed 10 March 2018.

xxxvii "Victoria". *Encyclopaedia Britannica.* **https://www.britannica.com/biography/Victoria-queen-of-United-Kingdom**. Accessed 10 March 2018.

xxxviii Widmer, Edward L. *Martin Van Buren: The American Presidents Series: The 8th President, 1837-1841.* 2003.

xxxix "Specie Circular". *Encyclopaedia Britannica.* **https://www.britannica.com/event/Specie-Circular**. Accessed 10 March 2018.

xl "Panic of 1837". *America's Library.* **http://www.americaslibrary.gov/aa/buren/aa_buren_panic_2.html**. Accessed 10 March 2018.

xli "Franklin D. Roosevelt". *Encyclopaedia Britannica.* **https://www.britannica.com/biography/Franklin-D-Roosevelt**. Accessed 10 March 2018.

xlii "Nathaniel Hawthorne". *Encyclopaedia Britannica.* **https://www.britannica.com/biography/Nathaniel-Hawthorne**. Accessed 10 March 2018.

xliii "Walt Whitman". *Encyclopaedia Britannica.* **https://www.britannica.com/biography/Walt-Whitman**. Accessed 10 March 2018.

[xliv] "Edgar Allan Poe". *Encyclopaedia Britannica.*
https://www.britannica.com/biography/Edgar-Allan-Poe. Accessed 10 March 2018.

[xlv]"American Anti-Slavery and Civil Rights Timeline." *US History.*
http://www.ushistory.org/more/timeline.htm. Accessed 10 March 2018.

[xlvi] "Abolitionism". *Encyclopaedia Britannica.*
https://www.britannica.com/topic/abolitionism-European-and-American-social-movement. Accessed 10 March 2018.

[xlvii] "John Adams". *Encyclopaedia Britannica.*
https://www.britannica.com/biography/John-Adams-president-of-United-States. Accessed 10 March 2018.

[xlviii] "Gag rule". *Encyclopaedia Britannica.*
https://www.britannica.com/topic/gag-rule. Accessed 10 March 2018.

[xlix] "Richard M. Johnson". *Encyclopaedia Britannica.*
https://www.britannica.com/biography/Richard-M-Johnson. Accessed 10 March 2018.

[l] "The Amistad case in fact and film." *History Matters.*
http://historymatters.gmu.edu/d/74. Accessed 10 March 2018.

[li] Widmer, Edward L. *Martin Van Buren: The American Presidents Series: The 8th President, 1837-1841.* 2003.

[lii] "Angelica Van Buren." *White House History.*
https://www.whitehousehistory.org/bios/angelica-van-buren. Accessed 10 March 2018.

[liii] "Dolley Madison." *Encyclopaedia Britannica.*
https://www.britannica.com/biography/Dolley-Madison. Accessed 10 March 2018.

[liv] Widmer, Edward L. *Martin Van Buren: The American Presidents Series: The 8th President, 1837-1841.* 2003.

[lv] "William Henry Harrison." *Encyclopaedia Britannica.*
https://www.britannica.com/biography/William-Henry-Harrison. Accessed 10 March 2018.

[lvi] "Sunday outing; house where the legacy of Van Buren lives on." *New York Times*. **https://www.nytimes.com/1991/11/10/travel/sunday-outing-house-where-the-legacy-of-van-buren-lives-on.html**. Accessed 10 March 2018.

[lvii] Widmer, Edward L. *Martin Van Buren: The American Presidents Series: The 8th President, 1837-1841*. 2003.

[lviii] "Martin Van Buren National Historic Site." *National Park Service*. **https://www.nps.gov/nr/travel/presidents/van_buren_lindenwald.html**. Accessed 10 March 2018.

[lix] "Abraham Lincoln." *Encyclopaedia Britannica*. **https://www.britannica.com/biography/Abraham-Lincoln**. Accessed 10 March 2018.

[lx] "James K . Polk." *Encyclopaedia Britannica*. **https://www.britannica.com/biography/James-K-Polk**. Accessed 10 March 2018.

[lxi] "Henry Clay." *Encyclopaedia Britannica*. **https://www.britannica.com/biography/Henry-Clay**. Accessed 10 March 2018.

[lxii] "Mexican-American War." *Encyclopaedia Britannica*. **https://www.britannica.com/event/Mexican-American-War**. Accessed 10 March 2018.

[lxiii] "Founding Fathers." *Encyclopaedia Britannica*. **https://www.britannica.com/topic/Founding-Fathers**. Accessed 10 March 2018.

[lxiv] "Revolutions of 1848." *Encyclopaedia Britannica*. **https://www.britannica.com/event/Revolutions-of-1848**. Accessed 10 March 2018.

[lxv] "California Gold Rush." *Encyclopaedia Britannica*. **https://www.britannica.com/topic/California-Gold-Rush**. Accessed 10 March 2018.

lxvi "Zachary Taylor." *Encyclopaedia Britannica.* **https://www.britannica.com/biography/Zachary-Taylor**. Accessed 10 March 2018.

lxvii Widmer, Edward L. *Martin Van Buren: The American Presidents Series: The 8th President, 1837-1841.* 2003.

lxviii Ibid.

lxix Ibid.

lxx Ibid.

lxxi "American Civil War." *Encyclopaedia Britannica.* **https://www.britannica.com/event/American-Civil-War**. Accessed 10 March 2018.

lxxii Widmer, Edward L. *Martin Van Buren: The American Presidents Series: The 8th President, 1837-1841.* 2003.

lxxiii "The 100 best novels: No 30 – The Red Badge of Courage by Stephen Crane (1895)." *The Guardian.* **https://www.theguardian.com/books/2014/apr/14/100-best-novels-red-badge-courage-stephen-crane**. Accessed 10 March 2018.

lxxiv "Confederate States of America." *Encyclopaedia Britannica.* **https://www.britannica.com/topic/Confederate-States-of-America**. Accessed 10 March 2018.

lxxv Widmer, Edward L. *Martin Van Buren: The American Presidents Series: The 8th President, 1837-1841.* 2003.

lxxvi Ibid.

lxxvii "Secession and the politics of the Civil War." *Encyclopaedia Britannica.* **https://www.britannica.com/place/United-States/Secession-and-the-politics-of-the-Civil-War-1860-65**. Accessed 10 March 2018.

lxxviii "Trail of Tears." *Encyclopaedia Britannica.* **https://www.britannica.com/event/Trail-of-Tears**. Accessed 10 March 2018.

[lxxix] "Ezra Pound." *Encyclopaedia Britannica.* **https://www.britannica.com/biography/Ezra-Pound**. Accessed 10 March 2018.

[lxxx] ""Thou Shalt Not", Said Martin Van Buren: Canto XXXVII". *Poetry Foundation.* **https://www.poetryfoundation.org/poetrymagazine/browse?contentId=20373**. Accessed 10 March 2018.

[lxxxi] "Gore Vidal." *Encyclopaedia Britannica.* **https://www.britannica.com/biography/Gore-Vidal**. Accessed 10 March 2018.

[lxxxii] Hummel, Jeffrey Rogers. "Martin Van Buren: The greatest American president. *The Independent Review.* **http://www.independent.org/pdf/tir/tir_04_2_hummel.pdf**. Accessed 10 March 2018.

[lxxxiii] "Van Buren's house is a home once more." *New York Times.* **https://www.nytimes.com/1988/06/02/garden/van-buren-s-house-is-a-home-once-more.html**. Accessed 10 March 2018.

[lxxxiv] "Dirty campaigns - a hallmark of U.S. history; Van Buren's precedent." *New York Times.* **https://www.nytimes.com/1988/11/20/opinion/l-dirty-campaigns-a-hallmark-of-us-history-van-buren-s-precedent-585488.html**. Accessed 10 March 2018.

[lxxxv] "Martin Van Buren – the original party boss." *New York Times.* **http://www.nytimes.com/2005/02/27/books/review/martin-van-buren-the-original-party-boss.html. Accessed 10 March 2018.**

CPSIA information can be obtained
at www.ICGtesting.com
Printed in the USA
BVHW051432250122
627119BV00004B/377